All Scripture references taken from the KJV of the Holy Bible, unless otherwise indicated.

When You Carried Me

by Dr. Marlene Miles

Freshwater Press 2024

freshwaterpress9@gmail.com

ISBN: 978-1-963164-44-2

Copyright 2024, Dr. Marlene Miles

All rights reserved. No part of this book may be reproduced, distributed, or transmitted by any means or in any form including photocopying, recording or other electronic or mechanical methods without prior written permission of the publisher except in the case of brief publications or critical reviews.

Table of Contents
Jesus Raises a Widow's Son 5

A Dead Man	9
Widows	16
Don't Cry	18
Jesus Touched It	22
Words Make the Man	33
I *Said*	35
He Had to Die	38
Back to His Mother	45
In Nain	47
He Touched *Me*	50
He Carried Me	60
Death, O Death	67
And They Praised God	74
Altars and Time	76
The Good Shepherd	79
He Laid It Down	85
Via Dolorosa	87
Dear Reader	93
Other books by this author	94

When You Carried Me

The words in this book
are provided by the Holy Spirit.
I pray you will be blessed.

Jesus Raises a Widow's Son

Soon afterward, Jesus went to a town called Nain, and his disciples and a large crowd went along with him.

As he approached the town gate, a dead person was being carried out—the only son of his mother, and she was a widow. And a large crowd from the town was with her.

When the Lord saw her, his heart went out to her and he said, **"Don't cry."**

Then he went up and touched the bier they were carrying him on, and the bearers stood still. He said, "Young man, I say to you, get up!"

The dead man sat up and began to talk, and Jesus gave him back to his mother.

> They were all filled with awe and praised God. "A great prophet has appeared among us," they said. "God has come to help his people."
>
> This news about Jesus spread throughout Judea and the surrounding country.
> (Luke 7:11-17)

The above Scripture story is about Jesus in a village called Nain. It is in the northern part of Israel, in Galilee, which is near where it borders Lebanon.

In the times of His ministry, Jesus didn't just stay on the main roads or linger in the larger cities; He took various routes to His destinations and encountered many people on the way to His bigger meetings. That means that no matter where you are or where you live, Jesus knows how to find you. Even if you live in a nowhere town out in the boonies, Jesus can find you.

Further, we ourselves cannot blindly miss the smaller highways and byways of life looking only for the big cities or the big opportunities. In small and quiet places God may have commanded a divine connection, opportunity, or a blessing for us.

In this town called Nain, Jesus raises to life the only son of a widow.

Nain, which means *green pastures*, or *lovely*, is only about a half a mile, from Shunem, where Elisha raised from the dead the son of a Shunamite woman in 2 Kings 4:31–37.

What was in the Old Testament is often echoed in the New Testament in Jesus' ministry, proving that Jesus did not come to do away with the Law, but to fulfill it. You see something in the Old Testament and it's a miracle? Then you see it in the New Testament; it's still a miracle. First God, by His Spirit, through the prophet, performed it in Shunem. Then Jesus, by His Word performed it in Nain. As in the Law of today, precedence has been set. Jesus said, **What I do; you shall do also, and even greater things.**

And Gehazi passed on before them, and laid the staff upon the face of the child; but there was neither voice, nor hearing. Wherefore he went again to meet him, and told him, saying, The child is not awaked. (2 Kings 4)

Elisha had been made aware that the woman's son was dead, so Elisha had sent

Gehazi over with the prophet's staff to resuscitate the boy. Sadly, it didn't work for Gehazi, and even sadder, it didn't work for the dead boy.

> And when Elisha was come into the house, behold, the child was dead, and laid upon his bed.
>
> He went in therefore, and shut the door upon them twain, and prayed unto the LORD.
>
> And he went up, and lay upon the child, and put his mouth upon his mouth, and his eyes upon his eyes, and his hands upon his hands: and stretched himself upon the child; and the flesh of the child waxed warm.
>
> Then he returned, and walked in the house to and fro; and went up, and stretched himself upon him: and the child sneezed seven times, and the child opened his eyes.
>
> And he called Gehazi, and said, Call this Shunammite. So he called her. And when she was come in unto him, he said, Take up thy son.
>
> Then she went in, and fell at his feet, and bowed herself to the ground, and took up her son, and went out. (2 Kings 4:31-37)

A Dead Man

Soon afterward, Jesus went to a town called Nain, and his disciples and a large crowd went along with him.

As he approached the town gate, a dead person was being carried out—the only son of his mother, and she was a widow. And a large crowd from the town was with her.
(Luke 7:11-12)

Nain, in a place of green pastures, which name means, *green pastures,* a man was being *put out to pasture*; he was dead.

There's a couple of ways of looking at this. Nain was a beautiful place, lovely, possibly like the Garden of Eden. When Adam and Eve died spiritually, they were put out of the Garden at Eden. This man had died physically from the Bible account. So, we see there are at least two ways to get put out of a beautiful place, a place of prosperity and all sufficiency. Die spiritually, or die physically. Or three ways, if both things happen.

This dead man was the only son of his mother, who was a widow – so that speaks to the man's approximate age. This dead man was probably not an old man because his mother was still alive. He may have been a young man. He was a man of a certain age who was not described as a *boy,* but Jesus had addressed him as *"young man."*

But he was dead.

He was not the only dead of this woman because she was a **widow**, so this means she had buried a husband. In those days a woman without a husband, single, unmarried, or widowed, there were certain stigmas attached. Married was the way of that day if you wanted to be respected.

Even in modern times, I've walked into a new church single, and I've walked in married; the treatment is different, but should it be? I've walked into the electronics store alone and been treated as an invisible person, but when a male of any variety accompanies me, suddenly we--, no, *he* gets all the help he needs without ever asking for it.

It's not as though many women in Bible days had productive jobs; their husbands took care of them, and they took care of the home. It is still that way in many cultures. So, if she was a widow then she was now depending on her only son all the more.

But he was dead, also.

Why were the men in her life dying? We don't know. Did she have anything to do with it? In many countries today the wife is the first suspect if a husband dies. To prove her innocence, she has to jump through a lot of hoops and do outrageous things. And a lot of what she has to do is occultic and superstitious.

Even in the USA, the boyfriend, girlfriend, or spouse is the first suspect if there is foul play. We should all be thankful for DNA to prove innocence when it should be proved. Thank God for CCTV and other surveillance instruments that we may detest, but that device can exonerate an innocent person by placing them away from a crime scene.

But her husband and son were both dead. Was there a family curse taking these men out? We don't know, but in cases of mysterious, sudden and untimely death, we should not only look in the natural, but we should also look to the spiritual, as well.

This woman was burying her son and there was a great company of people with her to either support her or they were friends with the deceased. Were they with her for encouragement, to pay respect, or to be nosey? We don't know.

How and when had the husband died? We don't know, the Bible doesn't say, but we know she was a widow.

The Bible is full of widows in which about 80 of them are mentioned. But then there is the issue of having to live *as a widow*. This happened to Jacob's concubines who slept with Reuben, the firstborn of Jacob was technically a prince, so if he called for the concubines to come to him, what options did they have?

Reuben chose to use the power and respect of his own birthright to sin. Not only that, but he also did it publicly. The way Reuben chose to use that authority is the same way he chose to lose it.

The power and respect of Reuben's birthright began to be in question. Now these women, even though they were obedient, have lost the respect of and the wifely position of their real husband, Jacob, as well. In Bible days, if a woman, whether the first wife, preferred wife, second wife, or handmaiden committed adultery, she was either put away, put out, and forced to live from then on as a widow. That's if she was lucky, some wives who were put away were stoned to death. Not much value was placed on women back then.

There are no accounts that I've seen of a man being stoned to death for adultery. King

David committed adultery, got Bathsheba pregnant and had her husband Uriah killed.

But as this fortunate and unfortunate woman was put away, that means she was not given a proper bill of divorcement. This means that no one else could legally marry her even if someone else wanted to, although she technically had no husband.

Few would want any of these situations – unless you've married the worst husband or wife ever. Unless you want to be rid of a *spirit spouse* then being a **spirit spouse widow** – hey, who wouldn't want that?

- Lord, kill every spirit spouse in my life no matter the source, origin or duration in my life, in the Name of Jesus.
- Lord, kill every spirit child from every entanglement with spirit spouse, in the Name of Jesus.
- Lord, kill every spirit spouse in my life no matter the source, origin or duration in my life, in the Name of Jesus.

- Lord, do not let me be put away by a spirit spouse, so that no one else will want me, in the Name of Jesus.

In the Courts of Heaven, I file for complete spiritual divorce, and I set *spirit spouse* ablaze with Holy Ghost Fire, in the Name of Jesus.

Widows

God has a special place in His heart for widows – natural, innocent widows, *real* widows. He forbids us to oppress widows and children. It is SAD that we have to be told this.

They devour widows' houses and for a show make lengthy prayers. These men will be punished most severely. (Mark 12:40)

Black widows, those who **make themselves** into widows, over and again. A black widow marries spouses to kill them, for gain. Many times, these are older very wealthy people who are murdered, but they don't have to be old.

Yes, I've watched too much ID Discovery, and I regret it, actually.

Historically, and criminally black widows are women who kill their own husbands. Their motives are varied, but usually it is for money.

Those who must *live as* widows was an Old Testament problem where if a woman was put away from her husband for adultery or any other reason, she would be forced to live as a widow – married, but not married, at the same time. No one wants that.

If married, you want to enjoy marriage and be successful in it, not put on a shelf.

Don't Cry

When the Lord saw her, his heart went out to her and he said, "Don't cry." (Luke 7:13)

Jesus came to Earth to bind up broken hearts. Immediately, Jesus' heart of compassion went out to this living woman, even though there was a dead man right there on a stretcher.

Don't cry.

Like Jesus said, to the widow woman, I say to you: *Don't cry.*

The anointing of God will bind up your broken heart and heal it. Whatever broke your heart, may the Lord deal with it for you so that you may heal and grow in the things of God. The Lord can deal with the dead, but He desires that the hearts of the living be healed and restored. Jesus spoke to the living woman first.

When the Lord saw her, his heart went out to her and he said, "Don't cry." (Luke 7:13)

Then he went up and touched the bier they were carrying him on, and **the bearers stood still.** (Luke 7:14)

Jesus touched what? Jews don't touch the dead or anything related to the dead. A bier is the funeral couch on which the Jews carry their dead on for burial. It's like a stretcher or a coffin???

Jesus touched it.

Anyone out in the open who touches someone who has been killed with a sword or someone who has died a natural death, or anyone who touches a human bone or a grave, will be unclean for seven days. (Numbers 19:16)

Jesus touched the bier, but the Scripture does not say that He touched the man. Jesus came to fulfill the law, not break it. Had He broken it, Jesus would have been unclean for seven days. Neither you nor I could even imagine Jesus sitting outside the gate, or locked away in His house for 7 days. No, that was not happening.

For the same reason, none of us can afford to be defiled or declared unclean for any period of time. For one, it embarrasses God. Second it keeps us from worshipping and serving God. It hinders our prayers. It makes us unavailable for ministry for the time of the defilement. Therefore, we observe the laws and rules of God, and we walk upright before Him and circumspectly in this world. We repent quickly and often, stay in the Word and stay prayerful.

Just this week a young girl told me the story of an entire wing of her school being locked down, but she had to leave school early to get to the appointment she was having with me. She pleaded with school officials, until they finally let her through. Down that hallway she saw the school nurse being taken out by EMS on a stretcher.

That she knew this was her school's nurse confirms that the woman wasn't dead, else her head would have been covered by a drape or a sheet. But the entire school was locked down so that she could be transported to the hospital.

How much more the Jews are adamant about not touching the unclean thing – the school didn't even want the kids to SEE the sick person.

Jesus Touched It

The funeral couch or bier on which the Jews carried their dead for internment was akin to a stretcher or coffin. Since it was associated with the dead man, only those bearing it should really touch it.

Christians don't adhere to such rules of cleanness and uncleanness, although maybe we should. Not just in the movies but sometimes in real life funerals there are many over emotional, super bereaved, and even hysterical attendees who kiss the dead, many touch the dead and some have tried to climb into the coffin with the dead.

There are so many wrong things that even Christians do regarding the dead, funerals and funeral rites. What are those things?

Don't take pictures at a funeral or burial service, even though everybody seems to be doing it these days. Some even make T-shirts and buttons and badges of the deceased; I've even seen images of the deceased in the coffin. Don't eat at a funeral. Don't take anything home from a funeral--, nothing. Don't put pictures of yourself or anyone else in the casket to be buried with the dead. Don't put the names of anyone else into the casket that will be buried. Yes, the person is dead, but earth will soon cover all of that; don't do it.

When you get home, don't go and tattoo the names and or faces of the dead on your body.

Jesus didn't touch that dead man, but He touched the funeral couch and in so doing, He transferred anointing, He transferred power.

Just as the woman with the issue of blood touched the hem of His garment; she did not actually touch Him, yet she was healed. Jesus transferred resurrection power to the dead man at Nain. He transferred healing power to the woman with the issue of blood.

We can take a lesson here. Jesus, the most powerful Altar was walking Galilee. Yes, there are living, moving breathing altars--, both good and bad. Jesus came upon the gate at a town called Nain. There was a laying to rest procession in progress. This is the same Jesus who said, **Let the dead bury the dead**, but Jesus was actually at a funeral in progress, and approached the funeral couch wherein the dead man lay. **He touched it.**

The funeral bed is itself an altar; anywhere there is something dead and blood has been shed, that also is an altar. Anything that requires worship and is an interface between the physical and spiritual world is an altar. There are many altars all around us, but none are more powerful than the Altar of Jesus Christ.

In Nain a most powerful altar walked up to a dead man on a bier, itself all an altar.

If a person can understand osmosis, the thing that is greater in intensity or concentration will flow into the thing that is lesser in concentration. Spiritually, the greater power will flow into the thing of lesser power if the power is allowed to flow, and if the receiver has faith to receive. If not, the greater power can dominate the lesser power if it chooses to and is not stopped.

Jesus came to Earth to die for us and to conquer Death. Death was the altar being serviced right there in Nain as Jesus came into town. That lesser altar could not contend against Jesus, it could not contaminate or defile Him; it could not make Him unclean, although Jewish law stated that is what would happen--, at least to the common man.

But this is Jesus we are talking about.

The large crowd of people with Jesus and the large crowd of people with the funeral were all there to witness the miracle of the man being raised from the dead. But is it not also a miracle that Jesus touched that bier on which the dead man lay but He, Himself did not become *unclean*?

Jesus, the most powerful Altar on Earth was showing His dominion over Death, and the formerly dead man arose as a testimony for the people --, those who believed, and those who would believe in the future.

The dead man of Nain arose and began to talk. He had to talk because they overcame by the Blood of the Lamb and the word of their testimony. When Jesus does anything for you, be sure to tell it. Testify of the goodness of the Lord in the land of the living.

Had Jesus touched the nurse's stretcher from that middle school the nurse could have received healing and gotten up from that mobile sick bed. The Spirit is that way.

Paul's handkerchiefs could heal.

Peter's shadow could heal.

See how the anointing flowed from the greater to the lesser, from the Apostles to the lay people who handled those items touched or carried by a man of high anointing?

Had anyone with the Spirit of God and intent with sufficient Love to make the gifts of healing work, and according to the faith of that nurse, might she not have been healed the moment she was touched to even be put on the stretcher by the paramedics?

This is how things of the Spirit work. God did it in the Old Testament through His prophets. Jesus did it in the New Testament by His words. Greater things shall you do also, since Jesus goes to the Father. Shouldn't doctors, nurses, EMS workers, and healthcare professionals be healers? They are fixers, but are they healers? Sadly, many don't even believe in God while they work on a multitude of people in distress and duress who are calling on God in their times of frustration, fear, and need.

Shouldn't Christians be healers? Yes, those were the gifts of healing. But if Jesus said greater things we can do. God did it. Jesus did it. We're following Jesus. He's doing what the Father does. Then we should be able to do what Jesus does. *Shouldn't Christians be healers?*

Because of the osmotic flow of anointing from the greater to the lesser, to the negative this is why you don't pick up things, put your hands on things, accept things, take things, wear things, eat things, drink things that you do not know the origins and the sources of. PERIOD. Yes, there is such a thing as spiritual transference. If you are dealing with things that are from a stronger altar than you serve, you will be susceptible to their intent against you.

It's embarrassing, but if witchcraft for example has attacked or afflicted you this means that the altar that is sending out that evil against you is stronger than you are. That's embarrassing, isn't it? Especially for Christians who say they don't believe in witchcraft and the like, but along comes some witchcraft that afflicts them or knocks them down because Christians who are supposed to be serving and connected to the highest Altar of all, are not, and they are weak.

Witches and agents of darkness may be stronger because they have greater sacrifices working on the evil altars they serve or priest at. By stronger sacrifices I mean just that. A witch or warlock may sacrifice any number of animals or things on their altar to send out curses to whomever they want to curse. For example, let's say they are sacrificing a cow to send out their evil from their evil altar. The value of that cow is anywhere from $1,000 to $2,500 but in some places that cow may be worth $3,500 to $5,000.

Yes, you are prayerful and crying out to God; you might even be fasting, but what sacrifice have you put on your altar or the altar you are seeking to connect with if you don't have an altar of your own?

You put $10 on that altar? Maybe $100?

Take this time to stop and think.

The Lord once showed me in the Spirit FOUR cows, four white Brahmin bulls for the sacrifice on an altar – AGAINST ME, for the kill. The Holy Spirit showed me that three had already been sacrificed and that's why I had been going through as I had, and that they (whoever *they* are) had one more and their intent was to kill. Saints of God, evil priests and priestesses, witches, warlocks, and some other "Christians" are not playing when they want something you have and/or want you dead.

Suffer not a witch to live (Exodus 22;18), but you'd better repent and cry for Mercy and be covered by the Blood of Jesus before you start your warfare.

Witchcraft can work even against Christians if you are not prayed up, if you are living in sin, or otherwise compromised because of bloodline iniquity, and/or if you have nothing on the Altar. Check yourself; I've had to.

If your car has no gas in it, you are going nowhere, outside of the Mercy of God. If your altar is cold with no sacrifice on it, what power will you have?

Witchcraft can work *through* Christians who are blind witches and they want what they want at any cost. We worry about fake friends, but a fake Christian is double jeopardy because if a person is not really who they are to you then there is no way their friendship can be real. Fake Christians or even ignorant Christians who don't know how to pray may propagate soulish, "I want" prayers and may actually be casting spells and performing the dark arts, unawares.

A pastor shared the story of how a very well off, influential friend of hers asked her to pray that a certain man become this friend's husband. Only problem was she failed to tell her praying pastor friend that the man was married with three children. Any prayer to take that man from his wife and family and make him marry the woman of wealth would be witchcraft.

If we are so bold to say, We don't believe in all that stuff, then we should be so bold as to be prayed up, read up in the Word, and fulfilling all we need to be doing in the Kingdom so our connection to the Altar of Jesus Christ is constant, strong, and secure. This will make us uncurse-able.

Words Make the Man

He (Jesus) said, "**Young man, I say to you, get up!**" Those are the words that Jesus used in this account. But the command to activate the anointing and the power of God to heal, raise up, or to make whole may vary; it is whatever the Spirit of God is saying to you at that exact moment. Say what the Holy Spirit tells you to say. When you are following in the footsteps of God, and of Jesus and you take dominion over any foul power, any evil *spirit*, even the *spirit of death,* say exactly what the Holy Spirit tells you to say; do not waver.

The dead man sat up and began to talk, and
Jesus gave him back to his mother.
(Luke 7:15)

I *Said*

The dialogue here is emphatic: **"Young man, I say to you, get up!"**

Had Jesus spoken previously to this dead man, and he hadn't responded?

Had Jesus called to Him from afar, before He had approached Nain or the gate of Nain?

Had Jesus called on this man while he was yet alive?

Why does it seem that there had been a reticence in answering Jesus? If someone said to you, **I SAY TO YOU** before issuing a command wouldn't you infer that they had spoken to you before and you either didn't hear, didn't obey, or both?

We mustn't be so hardheaded and hard of hearing when Jesus is calling us. When your momma calls you do you come running or hide? It depends, right? It depends on what you did or didn't do, did you break something, or did you not do your chores?
It depends on whether you have a good mom or not.

I again ask, had God already spoken to this man? And that man ignored God, perhaps more than once? Is that why he was dead? For Jesus to say, *I say to you*, speaks to rebelliousness, stubbornness, or hardheadedness.

When Jesus is calling us, it depends on the condition of our heart and the condition of our walk with Him as to whether we will answer, answer right away, hide, or try to hide if we are guilty, or if we have fear. Adam and Eve *hid* in the Garden when God came down to walk with them, as was His custom. But if we have love and we know **Him**, we know His voice we will answer right away.

Samuel was called of the Lord several times before he knew it was the Lord who was calling him; he thought it was Eli, the priest whom he was serving.

Until we become spiritually-minded, we will think that everything we do, or hear is from the physical and is only about the physical.

Jesus is calling you and that is a spiritual call. God sees us; Jesus is calling.

He Had to Die

God sees us in our polluted blood. In our sin. In our sin-sickness in our captivity, in our spiritual death—and He covers us. LOVE covers a multitude of sins…

We sin; He suffered.

We sin and He suffered.

We sin, yet He covers us.

We sin and we *feel* that we are suffering because there is punishment for sin and we don't want to go through anything. Even a child hates punishment of any kind. But as adult, Christian or fake Christian sinners the punishment we get is far less than it should be because of the Grace and Mercy of God. Still, we complain.

We should be thankful that God hasn't turned us over to Death. Even though we pay for sin, and it is painful, Jesus is still covering us because if He didn't, we'd be dead already.

In the shoot-em-up movies that many love, when there is a gunfight and a stand off, what does the combatant usually say? *"Cover me, I'm going in."*

The one who is offering cover is brave and may get shot because he is drawing fire to himself to keep the enemy from attacking the one who is "going in." My God of Mercy, isn't that what Jesus does for us? He covers us. He draws enemy fire *away* from us so we can escape like the bird from the fowler, and in the process, He may get wounded and bleed **for** us, so we can come out of captivity, come out of lockdown, come out of death and hell and the grave. Ultimately it is so we are the ones who are *"going in"*--, into the Kingdom of God. Hallelujah and Amen.

Joseph's brothers sinned – he suffered. Yes, Joseph is a type of Christ.

Joseph had to **die** out of the family, for a time, to save the Tribes of Israel – until such as a time as he could be put back with his family, a type of resurrection that led to restoration.

Joseph **carried** that family.

And in the carrying of that family look how many others were blessed and saved. Then and into the future wherever the 12 tribes of Israel would later become and grow to and go to, their descendants would be saved as well. Joseph **carried** them so he, like Jesus, but in a different way impacted the future and future generations. Amen.

As a teenager, the dream that God showed Joseph was that his family bowed to him. Even though in the dream he saw the sun and the moon, and 11 stars bowing to him, **the other brothers, <u>WERE ALSO STARS</u>**. Shall we not miss that, in the Name of Jesus. Amen. We should not try to undo God's anointed and appointed. Touch not God's anointed, do His prophets no harm. The brothers were also stars.

There is no record of Joseph trying to touch any of their anointing.

Even though he was bowed to, as in worshipped Joseph served and suffered, he served and he suffered, he served and suffered before he was honored and eventually worshipped, fulfilling his prophetic dreams.

How many folks want worship with no suffering? In the Old Testament the kings were the conquerors, they are the ones who went out to battle and risked life and limb; then they earned the right to rule.

Joseph's brother sinned: he suffered. Even in Joseph's suffering he *carried* his brothers and their generations.

We sin: Jesus suffered. And, in Jesus' suffering He carried all of us; He carried all of our sins to the Cross in a way that was true at Golgotha and still reaches into our generations today.

Can we not at least willfully suffer and bring our flesh under subjection to the Spirit of God by resisting the devil? Can we suffer in fasting, and prayers in the watches of the night, for instance? Those who don't suffer learn little, grow little, know little, and are usually not fit to rule and sometimes not even fit to serve.

I, myself have noticed that since I've gone through some things, and have gotten older, that I am easily touched by the conditions and infirmities of others. Years ago, my sister, Linda said that you cannot be impatient with people on the road and have road rage because you don't know the condition the driver is in. She added, *The driver could be sick, tired--, their leg could be hurting --, you just don't know what the driver is going through as to why they may be driving slowly that day.*

She was so right and that day because of her words I became a more compassionate driver.

Jesus was touched with the feelings of our infirmities. Of course, we may believe that Jesus being all man, but also all God didn't have disease, disorders, sicknesses, and syndromes but He came to Earth to experience what men go through on the day to day.

People are going through, every day. It's why there are drugs and alcohol usage and sometimes abuse because people are self-medicating for their aches, pains, heartaches, disappointments, and sadness over losses, for example. These people don't have Jesus in their lives to help them, heal them, and take the hurt away. Those who are saved and abuse any of these substances do not have **enough** Jesus in their life--, not because of any shortage in the Lord. Recall Jesus is the highest Altar; the anointing flows from the head, the beard, and even to the skirts of Aaron. The anointing is reachable and touchable; it flowed to the hem of Jesus' garment so that the weak woman with life draining out of her could touch it and be healed.

If they don't have enough anointing, it's not because Jesus is slack, it may be because they don't have the Spirit of God or walk in the Spirit to a degree that they lean on God instead of their own understanding.

Sometimes their own understanding is medicine, pills, drops, drugs, and alcohol. If one is leaning on natural solutions, he can not get the same results of one who is seeking spiritual solutions. The spiritual solution will solve every problem at its root and not merely treat symptoms.

Back to His Mother

He said, "Young man, I say to you, get up!"

The dead man sat up and began to talk, and Jesus gave him back to his mother.
(Luke 7:15)

Here, we reprint the verses from 2 Kings, where at the end Elisha had Gehazi to call the boy's mother, then the mother took the boy and went out.

Then he returned, and walked in the house to and fro; and went up, and stretched himself upon him: and the child sneezed seven times, and the child opened his eyes.

And he called Gehazi, and said, Call this Shunammite. So he called her. And when she was come in unto him, he said, Take up thy son.

Then she went in, and fell at his feet, and bowed herself to the ground, and took up her son, and went out. (2 Kings 4:35-37)

  The echoing of giving the boy or man back to his mother is symbolic of each of those males being born again. After rigorous labor and childbirth one of the first things the doctor, nurse, doula, or midwife will do is give the child to his mother.

  When Jesus raised anyone from the dead it is a type of rebirth, being born again and anew. In a hospital or other birthing room, the father could be present, but the baby is given to its mother, first.

In Nain

He said, "Young man, I say to you, get up!"

The dead man sat up and began to talk, and Jesus gave him back to his mother. (Luke 7:15)

Jesus was able to do this because before the foundation of the world, the Lamb had already been slain. Jesus had **already suffered**, He was just on Earth to walk it through, to walk out what had already happened in the Spirit.

The people praised the LORD. But can you imagine walking along in a funeral procession but then all of a sudden there is no funeral because the dead man is now alive again? That might take a moment, but eventually you would praise God because --, how else could this happen? It's not just that the man is dead, but the mother is grieving and others are in their stages of grief--, disbelief, blame, denial-, whatever stage they are in, but suddenly the man is alive again. Can you imagine how they have to be jolted into rational thinking again?

If these were very superstitious people, they either may not believe their eyes, or they may suspect some funny business. Of course, Jesus didn't cast out devils by demonic means and the resurrection power that God gave Jesus is 100% God.

In today's world, if you see such a thing on deliverance grounds and in witchcraft circles suspect foul play and demonic activity because to see someone who is supposed to be dead walking around as if they are living is surely not of God.

He Touched *Me*

Well, saints of GOD, when we were deep in sin and trespasses, laying in our own polluted blood, we were **dead**.

He touched me. Jesus touched me – we often have cried out for a *Touch* from the Master. Even in our sin and pollution, in our sin sickness, and being spiritually dead, the only hope of resurrection and restoration is Jesus Christ. Amen.

We cry out for a touch, yet we are not worthy, and we are asking the Lord again to touch the unclean thing – **us**. To touch the dead thing.

We have sinned. All have sinned.

If we had rejected our Father to do this sin, these sins, we made ourselves spiritually fatherless, unless you count letting Satan be the father to our lies, rebellion, and indiscretions.

No Christian wants Satan for a father.

Malachi 4 talks about turning the heart of the child back to the father and the Father back to the child, lest He smite the Earth with a curse:

> And he shall turn the heart of the fathers to the children, and the heart of the children to their fathers, lest I come and smite the earth with a curse. (Malachi 4:6)

When we reject Jesus who prophetically is and is to be our Husband – as the church we become willful widows or spinsters--, those who never marry. Five of the 10 who did not trim their lamps sealed their own fate by making themselves husbandless.

When we reject our husbands, we make ourselves into widows, in a sense. And vice versa, men who reject their wives, become widowers. Man, if you have a wife but you reject your wife, then you technically *put yourself away* because you are still married, but not living a successful and happy married life.

- Lord, forgive me, if I have made myself into a widow or a widower, in the Name of Jesus.

Widows / widowers who have rejected God or been put away because of sin will raise what kind of sons? If you've been *put away* because of adultery and fornication – no one wants you because of your sinning against God really, but they see it as sinning against them. Again- what kind of son will you raise if you **reproduce** after your *kind*? If your *kind* is the sinful kind, a son with no Godly spiritual covering, no father or no spiritual Father, that son will be at risk of being *taken out* on a stretcher, a gurney, or on a bier of the spiritual or physical kind.

I once dated a fellow who stopped dating me because of the mess he felt he had made of his life. He even stated to me that no "decent" person would want him now. I didn't have any idea what he was talking about until about three months later the rumor mill churned some gossip my way. This fellow was pregnant out of wedlock.

Aww --, he considered me someone decent. But I didn't reject him. I didn't feel that way toward him, but he felt condemned by his own sin and counted himself out of my life. This man was saved. He had a natural father and mother, but by choosing to sin had he rejected their teachings and made himself temporarily, at least, fatherless, and motherless? Had he rejected the Word of God and made himself also spiritually Fatherless?

No wonder he felt so bad.

If he had not yet repented of being Fatherless, without God is like death itself. Look at what Jesus went through on the Cross.

My Father, why hast Thou rejected me?

About three in the afternoon Jesus cried out in a loud voice, *"Eli, Eli lema sabachthani?"* (which means "My God, my God, why have you forsaken me?"), (Matthew 27:46)

Because of sin. It's in the Bible.

Repent. Turn back to God and He will turn back to you.

Don't let condemnation take you out of relationship with God. Don't let condemnation take you out of relationships with people; you may be breaking off divine connections, unawares. Don't let condemnation take you out, after all, it is the last step before destruction. Don't do that to yourself. Don't let the enemy do that to you. Jesus will save you, cleanse you, heal you. He can restore even the mess you may have made or think you have made of your life. The Holy Spirit will bring you to conviction so you can repent, but He does not bring you to condemnation; that is devil work. If you are receiving thoughts or words of condemnation—that is not GOD. That is not Jesus. **THAT IS NOT THE HOLY SPIRIT.**

That is the devil.

When we were lost in sin, dead in sin, the Word of the Lord came whether we know that we heard it or not. We heard it; our spirit man heard it. Our spirit man can hear the tiniest voice and thank God because sometimes we lack boldness and our own voices are tiny, yet God hears us.

Maybe the call came but we didn't answer, or we answered in the physical and like Samuel the first three times and in so doing, answered the wrong *person*. If that was you and there was no Eli in your life to tell you that was God, you may have erred; you may have dismissed that *call*, thinking it was your imagination, or that it was nothing. When really, if it was God, it was **EVERYTHING**.

Until we become spiritually-minded we won't know or even suspect that it is Jesus, not a physical person who is calling.

Jesus is calling.

Jesus is calling. Jesus stands at the door and knocks. Do we not hear it? Do we not *want* to hear it? Do we pretend not to hear it? Are we afraid because of our own guilt? Are we so rebellious we don't want to stop sinning, yet?

Or, are the *spirits* that are in us running this and will not let us answer?

- Lord set us free from all spiritual oppression and possession, in the Name of Jesus.

Have we become spiritually minded yet so we can know this is **God** who is calling and not a physical person?

Jesus is calling. He is calling your name. He is calling you out of whatever you are in--, captivity, sin, feelings of condemnation, or darkness. He is calling. Do you not answer or are there too many other voices? Do you not answer because you don't know Him or that it is Him--, yet? Then ask,

- Jesus is that You? Let it only be You, Lord who calls me, who calls my name, in the Name of Jesus.

If you are being called out of sin, unrighteousness, captivity, hell, death, and the grave it can only be Jesus. He will call you out of sickness, loss, failure, defeat, and disappointment. He will call you out of loneliness, unhappiness, and darkness, into His marvelous Love and Light.

He will call you for life and that more abundantly. Yes, He chastises those whom He loves, but that chastisement lasts but a moment, in the scheme of things. Anything else, anything more is abuse and that is not of God.

Jesus calls us, and if He has to say, **I say to you**, He will do it, but that usually means that He has been calling and you didn't hear, or didn't acknowledge, or worse, didn't listen, or didn't obey.

If He has to say,

- I SAY TO YOU, GET UP.
- I SAY TO YOU, GET UP.
- I SAY TO YOU, GET UP OUT OF YOUR POLLUTED BLOOD, GET UP OUT OF YOUR WRETCHED, SINFUL LIFE, GET UP AND LIVE, He will do it.

Then He may ask, ***Where's your mother?*** There is a thing about calling on mother coming and going. In the news a man who was killed by the police was heard calling on his mother. Little children and old people call on mother. To the newborn, the dying, and the born again: ***Where is your mother?***

Jesus gave the man back to his mother; I suspect because the man's father was dead and the man needed nurturing or more upbringing. The Shunamite woman's son that Elisha raised was given to his mother; he could have been of tender age since he was described as a *boy* and definitely needed more care.

He Carried Me

When we were lost in sin, Jesus **carried** us.

When Jesus touched the bier, the men who carried it <u>**stopped.**</u> When they stopped carrying the man, that's when Jesus *carried* that man who was dead and being funeralized that day. But Jesus obeyed Jewish law and did not touch the dead man, physically. Jesus carried that dead man, **with His words.** When we were spiritually dead and in captivity, the devil had a funeral bier ready for us, but Jesus said, **No!** Jesus would not want any of us to die prematurely, and He doesn't want any of us to die *in sin.* **In sin** means there is no chance for repentance and it's straight to hell after death.

The Words of the Lord are powerful; they are Spirit, and they are life. The Words that Jesus speaks they are life. The favor of God is life. When the Lord but looks on you; that is life. When the Lord approaches you, even a dead man--, that is life. When the Lord sees you, even in polluted blood, or already on a funeral stretcher—the doctor has already *called it* and signed the certificate, but Jesus is looking on you--, that's life. Man has given up on you, but Jesus is the Way, the Truth, and the Life.

You've been that dead man.

I've been that dead man. Spiritually dead--, either of us, or both of us. We don't even know each other, but may have fallen to the same fate as did Adam and Eve--, spiritually dead. The devil had sent men in with stretchers to carry the body to wherever he thought he could abscond with it, but Jesus said, **NO; wait**. Or, Jesus said, **No, not yet.**

Jesus can't touch the unclean thing, with His hands, as we are instructed not to touch the dead thing, but with the living words, the proceeding words, the prophetic words, the Spirit-filled words of Jesus the spirit of man is lifted, resuscitated, revived, and resurrected.

Our own spirit grows by the Word of God. We read the Word; faith comes by hearing. We feed our spirit man the Word. Jesus is the Word, and if the Word is speaking the Word, how can we not be but edified and revived?

If Jesus says, **Get up and Live**, your spirit man must obey. **Get up, and Live. Get up out of your polluted blood, and live.**

You have been that dead man before.

I've been that dead man; but Jesus came. And Jesus either touched the couch we were dead on, or touched us, or simply lifted us from where we lay and *carried* us with His Word(s).

Jesus came to defeat Death, and this was a foretaste of Glory Divine. Every time He raised someone from the dead, it was a foretelling of His own resurrection, and a marker that He is able, it is a testimony of what He has done, <u>and</u> can do for us.

When we were dead in sin, Jesus **carried** us. Had He not we would not be alive today. If a man had carried us, he would have taken us straight to that hole in the ground and we would have been buried already.

If the devil carried us, we would be in hell already. You know how they say don't kick a man when he's down? Vultures and the devil rush in when a man is down.

Jesus comes in to rescue and save when a man is down. Jesus *carried* us in our pollution, in our sin-sickness & and in our spiritual death, so we could be revived, resuscitated, renewed, restored, re-gened, and live to tell about it in the Land of the Living. Amen.

Jesus *carried* our sin to the Cross.

Jesus *carried* our burdens.

Jesus *carried* our iniquity.

Jesus *carried* our pollution.

Jesus *carried* our diseases and afflictions.

Jesus *carried* our Death to the Cross. We should have been the ones gone; but He gave up the Ghost. Whatever was ours or was because of our own doing that Jesus carried, it represents us. Therefore, if Jesus carried any part of us, or any part of our doings, He *carried us.* This is how altars work, when anything that represents you is on the altar, it is the same as **you** being on the altar.

Jesus came to defeat Death and He **did**.

Think about this: Death has to be a real *mamma jamma* for Jesus to have to come to Earth and do all that he did to **DEFEAT IT**.

We sin; He suffered.

We cut ourselves or carelessly allow ourselves to be cut; He ***bleeds.***

We hide *to* sin or *from* sin, or because *of* sin, but He comes to find us; He does not want that one should be lost.

We get broken hearts because of wrong choices, and He binds our broken hearts, to heal us and restore our souls.

We make ourselves sick, with sin; He **takes** our suffering away. He wipes away our tears; He heals us.

We get ourselves captive or locked up; He comes as the King of Glory, as the Lord Sabaoth to set us free.

Knowingly or unknowingly, we help the devil do works of darkness in the Earth. Because the devil has no physical body to do things in the Earth, he tricks, bribes, deceives, employs or hires humans to do it. Jesus helps us to undo the works of darkness that we've foolishly, rebelliously embarked upon. Jesus came to destroy the works of the devil.

- Lord, like little children making mistakes all the time, forgive us, in the Name of Jesus.
- Lord, forgive us for giving You so much work to do. Forgive us because You have the power to forgive, in Jesus' Name.
- Lord, with a heart of compassion, which **You** gave us, forgive us that we have done and do **so much evil** that You had to come and die for us, in the Name of Jesus.

Death, O Death

O death, where is thy sting? O grave, where is thy victory?

The sting of death is sin; and the strength of sin is the law. (1 Corinthians 15:55-56)

Death surely stung the Shunamite woman whose boy was dead. Death stung the widow of Nain whose husband was dead; now her only son was dead, also. Surely these people were in the pains of grief at their times of loss, when Elisha and then Jesus came along, respectively.

Jesus went to hell, took captivity captive, and gave gifts unto men. If defeating Death and taking captivity captive are in the same story—Jesus' story, might that not tell us that we definitely don't want to be captive?

Death is the sequela of captivity. Death is the purpose of captivity--, if not death of the person, death of something about that person's life or godliness.

Captivity means that the person, or if the person is still alive, some *part* of the person is being held and usually tormented in some region of hell. Captivity happens to the living while they are yet alive.

Who would want hell on Earth, as they say? But that is captivity.

Who would want to be alive, believe they are alive, but have part of their being or soul sequestered in hell?

Captivity shows itself in a person when they are doing, thinking, saying ungodly things, whether they say they are saved, or not-

-, but especially when they are *not* saved. The devilish, demonic, unpleasant things that men do and do to one another is because demons have captured their soul and changed the programming from what God installed in them and intended that they become and do.

Let's say you like to keep your channel on worship stations or preaching channels; you praise the Lord, day and night and you bless the saints left and right. But suddenly your modus operandi has changed. You are now acting out nighttime dramas, crime shows, and other flesh acts that you really want to do in the dark and hide in the dark. **Your channel has been changed. <u>That is captivity.</u>** Stuff in your life that normally works suddenly doesn't work anymore--, that is captivity.

Shakespeare said that the whole world is a stage, and every person is acting out their "part." When your soul is captured, unless you are locked away and do nothing at all--, and that is sometimes the plan of the enemy, you will be behaving as a different man in order to fulfill evil, if you are not inherently evil.

Old Testament Saul was turned into a new man--, *often*. Saul was very susceptible to the *spirits*-, too much, actually. To his good, when Saul was in the company of the prophets he prophesied. But when King Saul was alone, he could easily become oppressed or overcome by evil *spirits* that made him violent and sent him into homicidal rages that lasted for days.

Saints of God, when we are oppressed by evil *spirits*, those *spirits* are in our soul, and they talk. They talk, they talk, they spout their own doctrine to indoctrinate man, to influence man to make that man take on the nature of that devil, that demon, that evil *spirit*. When that man acts out based on what the evil *spirit* is influencing him to do it is as though he is tossed about. Tossed about by winds of doctrine, *internally*.

If evil *spirits* are in your soul, running their mouth, especially, that is its own form of captivity. You have been boarded by enemy combatants--- it is still captivity, yet you are moving about the planet, you think you are acting in your own free will and on your own accord; but you are not, not really, or not completely. You are in captivity.

Who in their right mind would want to be in jail – spiritual jail or any other? Who in their right mind could be content to be captive?

Wherefore he saith, When he ascended up on high, he led captivity captive, and gave gifts unto men.

(Now that he ascended, what is it but that he also descended first into the lower parts of the earth?

He that descended is the same also that ascended up far above all heavens, that he might fill all things.) Ephesians 4:8-10

"O Death, where is your sting? O Hades, where is your victory?" The sting of death is sin, and the strength of sin is the law. But thanks be to God, who gives us the victory through our Lord Jesus Christ. (1 Corinthians 15:55-58 NKJV)

For as in Adam all die, even so in Christ shall all be made alive. (1 Corinthians 15:22)

For he must reign, till he hath put all enemies under his feet. The last enemy that shall be destroyed is death. (1 Corinthians 15:25-26)

Not like Kenny on SouthPark, who dies every episode, but have you any idea how many times you've died from sin--, how many times you have killed things in your life because of sin and had to call on the LORD to help you, save you, save that thing, or correct that issue? How many times have you needed deliverance? How many times have you needed it? How many times have you needed restoration? How many times has something in your life had to be made alive, quickened by the Lord Jesus Christ?

Thirty-nine times? Once for every lash across Jesus' back?

Seventy times seven? the number of times we are told to forgive in a day?

How many times?

How many times?

Lord, You know.

If we had 10,000 tongues it wouldn't be enough to say, THANK YOU.

O death, where is thy sting? O grave, where is thy victory? The way that question is put tells us that Jesus made a public spectacle of death –so we all would know that Death has been defeated. Amen.

And having spoiled principalities and powers, he made a shew of them openly, triumphing over them in it.
(Colossians 2:15)

The sting of death is sin; and the strength of sin is the law.

But thanks be to God, which giveth us the victory through our Lord Jesus Christ.

Therefore, my beloved brethren, be ye stedfast, unmoveable, always abounding in the work of the Lord, forasmuch as ye know that your labour is not in vain in the Lord. (1 Corinthians 15:56-58)

And They Praised God

They were all filled with awe and praised God. "A great prophet has appeared among us," they said. "God has come to help his people." This news about Jesus spread throughout Judea and the surrounding country. (Luke 7:16-17)

      That is a wonderful praise to the Lord, but the miracle of restoring life to a dead man who was on the way to be put into the ground is indeed a miracle. It is not a normal expectation of God--, or is it? *Help* to these people meant resurrection? Praise God for Jesus and thank God for resurrection power. These people must have had amazing levels of faith to think this is an everyday occurrence. Still, Jesus carried that widow's son from the grips of death back to the land of the living.

Jesus carried our sin. Jesus carried my sin, and *your* sin to the Cross.

Altars and Time

In order for Jesus to carry all that sin to the Cross, the dimension of Time must be addressed. Jesus is He who was and is and is to come. Jesus is everlasting. Of course, Jesus transcends space and time, most likely because He has authority over both. Time must obey the Lord. Didn't God make time stand still for Joshua as he fought the Battle of Gibeon in his quest for Canaan?

That Blood-soaked Cross still speaks generations later. Jesus, who is that perfect and blemish free sacrifice made an Altar that is not subject to Time.

Most altars are not subject to time unless they are being torn down, prayed against, smashed with the Thunder Hammer of God, or burned to ashes by Holy Ghost Fire. That is when they become subject to time. They are subject to time at the time that you are doing spiritual warfare against them and tearing them down, as the Word instructs.

The component of Time not being addressed is one of the reasons why ancient altars from your father's house or from anywhere could still be emanating against you and your bloodline. As long as someone is priesting at that altar, ministering at that altar, offering sacrifice, praise and worship, that altar will still speak and emanate curses if it is an evil altar.

If it is not an evil altar it can send blessings out to you and your bloodline. The Altar of Jesus Christ, the Altar of the Lord should be the predominant Altar speaking into and over your life and that of your bloodline. The fact that Jesus could transcend space and Time, and do that means that blood can do that.

It also means that sin and the iniquity of sin also can do that. Anything spiritual can do that.

Blood is spiritual.

Additionally, witches and warlocks can work outside of Time.

You'd better get spiritually minded so you can address matters that have a Time component to them, so you can speak to Time and have it work for you and not against you, in Jesus' Name.

The Good Shepherd

We may recall the image of Jesus carrying the lost sheep that He has gone out, even into the wilderness to locate. Illustrated Bibles often show Jesus with the sheep or carrying one across His shoulders. That is a sweet and comforting image. We may want to think that is how Jesus carries us.

I am the good shepherd: the good shepherd giveth his life for the sheep. John 10:11

I am the good shepherd, and know my sheep, and am known of mine.

As the Father knoweth me, even so know I the Father: and I lay down my life for the sheep.

And other sheep I have, which are not of this fold: them also I must bring, and they shall hear my voice; and there shall be one fold, and one shepherd.

Therefore doth my Father love me, because I lay down my life, that I might take it again.

No man taketh it from me, but I lay it down of myself. I have power to lay it down, and I have power to take it again. This commandment have I received of my Father. (John 10:14-18)

Jesus *carried* me, when He came looking for me and finally found me in the Wilderness--, the Wilderness of my own life and lying in my polluted blood. The Wilderness is where people die. The Wilderness is where people go to die.

Jesus picked me up and carried me out of the Wilderness, back to safety. Whether He picked me up physically like our Sunday School pictures or if the sheer power of the

Word of God called me, lifted me, saved me, chose me and brought me back into the fold – it doesn't matter, I was *carried*. But in my polluted blood and the pollution of the blood of my family bloodline, blood was sure to be somewhere or everywhere.

By His stripes we were healed. Jesus picked me up, bound my broken heart and healed it. Jesus restored my soul. Jesus bled for me so **my** own bleeding could stop. The life is in the blood, therefore because of His heart of compassion toward me, toward us all, we are hurt, we are cut, but He is bleeding *for us*.

Forgiveness is bloody.

Because of Jesus' heart of compassion when He sees me, He says to any part of me that is still alive, **"Don't cry."** Crying involves tears, but the blood also cries. He says, **"Don't cry,"** and the tears stop, the bleeding ceases; we live again. To our ears, Jesus may as well say, **Don't die.**

By crying, by bleeding all the life is leaking out of you. Don't die. Jesus binds the broken hearts and stops the bleeding because the demons want blood; they see it as you sacrificing to them.

Instead: listen to Jesus as He says to you and/or your spirit man: **Don't bleed. Don't cry. Don't die.** Whatever Jesus says, the words of the Lord are pure words: as silver tried in a furnace of earth, purified seven times, (Psalm 12).

In the Book of Luke, Chapter 7, the formerly dead man sat up and began to talk, proving that even though he was born again and given again to his mother, he is not a baby all over again.

What might a formerly dead, just risen to life again man say? What might he have to say? Would anyone hear him? I believe he'd have a lot to say, mostly praises unto Our God. I also believe that many would hear and believe him.

Receive the sign, wonder, and miracle, or *become* it.

When we've been on that funeral bier spiritually speaking, when we've been spiritually dead Jesus walked up and touched the funeral bier so we would not end up on a funeral pyre. So we wouldn't end up being buried, so we wouldn't end up also dead physically.

How many times has that happened to any one of us?

How many times?

Lord, you know.

Some of those times we have called on the Lord to help us, save us, deliver us. Some of those times it was by His great Mercy because we may not have even been saved yet. On the Cross Jesus said, **Father, forgive them they know not what they do.** Remember, Jesus is an altar, remember the Words He speaks are Spirit, and they are life. Remember His Words do not die; His words do not fall to the ground, His words do not return void, but they perform what He purposes for them to accomplish.

Lord, forgive them, they know not what they do.

So, in the midst of our ignorance, not having a clue as to what we are doing, the forgiveness and Mercy of God that Jesus spoke on our behalf, hanging on that Cross, that Altar is still speaking today.

For those of us who are saved and know much better, recall that judgment begins in the House of the Lord, so if you don't know better, learn better, get better, do better, in the Name of Jesus. God is merciful but He says that His Spirit will not always strive with man.

He Laid It Down

Joseph was put in a pit and sold against his will – that is how he lost the life that he knew as a boy, but later when his family came to him, he was restored in relationship with them.

Jesus *willfully* laid down more than one life. The first life He laid down was the life that He knew in Glory with His Father, God to come here as a man and to save us.

No man taketh it from me, but I lay it down of myself. I have power to lay it down, and I have power to take it again. This commandment have I received of my Father. (John 10:18)

He then later laid down His Earth life to be restored back to His Father, God, our Father. Note at that time, He gave His mother, Mary, over to the care of one of His Disciples. He was not here for Earth restoration for Himself, but He carried our sins to the Cross so that we could be restored back to the Father and with one another in the faith.

Remember, it's so the children can return to the Father and the Father to the children, so God doesn't have to smite the Earth with a curse. (Malachi 4:6)

Via Dolorosa

> Surely he hath borne our griefs, and carried our sorrows: yet we did esteem him stricken, smitten of God, and afflicted.
> (Isaiah 53:4)

Jesus carried my sins; He carried your sins; He carried the sin of the whole world. Jesus went by the *Via Dolorosa,* the Way of Suffering. The Lamb had already been slain before the foundation of the world, but Jesus had to come to walk this thing out--, literally.

The path that Jesus took, the Via Dolorosa was planned out by the Roman soldiers. He carried his own heavy cross on the way to His crucifixion. That cross weighed as much as 160 pounds, weighing as much as a fully grown man.

In the Old City of Jerusalem, the Via Dolorosa is about a half mile long. I've walked it and it is roughly cobbled with old stones and while not carrying anything at all it is hard to get one's footing there. So, you can imagine if you are carrying something heavy and cumbersome how hard it would be to walk those cobblestones. The cobblestones historically made traction easier for horses, but not for man. Old stones do present stumbling blocks for men in this life, as we are all called to be lively stones, and not dead weight.

That cross that Jesus carried and was eventually crucified on and died on represented the weight of one man— with all his sin. Jesus carried it spiritually as well, so it represented the sins of one man.

But at the same time, it represented every man, and all the sins of every man.

And at the same time, it spoke through Time to speak for and save every man from that moment on, until Jesus returns again. Amen.

In the Old Testament era, Romans had a practice of strapping a dead body to a criminal. When a man murdered another that dead man was strapped to the perpetrator's back until the perpetrator was also dead. That criminal was forced to live out their last few weeks in a walking punishment by carrying a maggot-infested corpse strapped to their bare back. During the process of the cadaver's decomposition, it slowly leaked poisons into the criminal, making them sicker and sicker by the day, until they finally died a very slow, painful death.

Jews, as you recall were not to touch any dead person or any unclean thing, so to have a dead body touching a person, was the epitome of reproachment, ostracizing, estrangement, abandonment, and a very lonely, loveless, friendless, people-less, and Godless death.

God on the other hand is full of Mercy and forgiveness. Moses killed a man but still led the Hebrews out of bondage in Egypt. God did not strap that dead man to Moses' back until Moses also succumbed; He forgave Him.

The Romans were cruel and ungodly. They practiced condemnation rather than forgiveness. They were very much like the devil. The devil will entice you to sin, all to entrap you into punishment, condemnation, and death.

God says something like, **They sinned, bring them under conviction and if they repent, and turn back to Me, I will forgive them.**

The devil says, *Gotcha!*

A sin-free man was accused, tried, and wrongfully convicted of everyman's sin, and all that sin was strapped to His back, where He was to carry it unto death by way of the *Via Dolorosa*. This wasn't to be the slow death of having a dead man literally strapped to His back, which would have been impossible anyway because Jesus had killed no one. But death was sped up though, as He **was put on a Cross to die of asphyxiation.**

This sin-free man who gave up the Ghost more than 2000 years ago has *already* carried your sin to the Cross. He already had dead weight, a dead body, a corpse put on His back which was Roman custom in that day.

This event already happened before **you** ever happened, before all of your ancestors except for 2 or a few of them had already been born and accepted Him or rejected Him, sinned, or tried not to sin at least. It happened before they believed in Him, believed on Him--, or didn't.

Jesus carried ALL of that!

And, what *weight* was that?

How much blood was that?

Jesus carried us all prophetically, spiritually and in this example, literally not just to the Cross, He carried the Cross.

That cross was *me*. While I had no reason to be cross with Jesus. While I may not have heard or listened to Him calling me. While I may have run out into the Wilderness and gotten lost on my own, or even tried to hide from Him and couldn't make my way back. He came to get me and put me on His back, not as the bleating, little Lamb, but as the fully grown, lifeless, fully-weighted being that death and hell were pulling on gravitationally to make me weigh even more than I did. I was across His back, but He had stopped my bleeding and He had taken it with 39 lashes across His own flesh.

Lord, I was that dead weight across Your back. Thank God for salvation; now I live.

Lord, I was the reason You had to bleed.

Lord, I was that dead man strapped to Your back. yet You were innocent; You committed no sin. You committed no crime. You did absolutely nothing to me; You only came here, to the Wilderness of Earth, *for* me.

Lord, I thank You, please forgive me, in the Name of Jesus.

Thank YOU, LORD JESUS for when you **carried** me.

Amen.

Dear Reader

My God of Mercy.

God of peace sanctify you through and through, in Jesus' Name.

I bless you, in the Name of Jesus.

Amen.

Dr. Marlene Miles

Other books by this author

(related or mentioned titles are pictured with links)

AK: The Adventures of the Agape Kid

AMONG SOME THIEVES

Ancestral Powers

Blindsided: *Has the Old Man Bewitched You?*

https://a.co/d/5O2fLLR

Churchzilla, The Wanna-Be, Supposed-to-be Bride of Christ

Darkness

Demons Hate Questions

Devil Weapons: Unforgiveness, Bitterness,…

Dream Defilement https://a.co/d/4f4P3Et

Don't Refuse Me, Lord (4 book series)

Every Evil Bird

Evil Touch

Failed Assignment

Fantasy Spirit Spouse

FAT Demons (The): *Breaking Demonic Curses*

The Fold (4 book series)

- The Fold (Book 1)
- Name Your Seed (Book 2)
- The Poor Attitudes of Money (3)
- Do Not Orphan Your Seed

got HEALING? Verses for Life

got LOVE? Verses for Life

got HOPE? Verses for Life

got money?

How to Dental Assist

How to Dental Assit2: Be Productive, Not Wasteful

Irresistible: The Triumphal Entry of Jesus

 https://a.co/d/9qumQbQ

Let Me Have A Dollar's Worth

Living for the NOW of God
https://a.co/d/1pwGkJJ

Lose My Location https://a.co/d/crD6mV9

Man Safari, *The (mini book)*

Marriage Ed. Rules of Engagement & Marriage Made Perfect in Love

Motherboard (The) - soul prosperity series

Plantation Souls

Power Money: Nine Times the Tithe

The Power of Wealth *(forthcoming)*

Seasons of Grief

Seasons of War

Sift You Like Wheat

Soul Prosperity soul prosperity series 3
https://a.co/d/5p8YvCN

Souls Captivity soul prosperity series 2

The Spirit of Poverty

This Is NOT That: How to Keep Demons from Coming At You

Throne of Grace: Courtroom Prayer

Time Is of the Essence   https://a.co/d/1w4V5o9

Too Many Wives: *Why You Have Lady Problems*

Tormenting Spirits   https://a.co/d/dAogEJf

Triangular Power *(series)*

- Powers Above
- SUNBLOCK
- Do Not Swear by the Moon
- STARSTRUCK

Uncontested Doom

Upgrade: How to Get Out of Survival Mode

- **Toxic Souls** (Book 2 of series)
- **Legacy** (Book 3 of series)

Warfare Prayer Against Beauty Curses

Warfare Prayer Against Poverty

What Have You to Declare?

When the Devourer is Rebuked (mini book)

When You See Blood https://a.co/d/apvdjvW

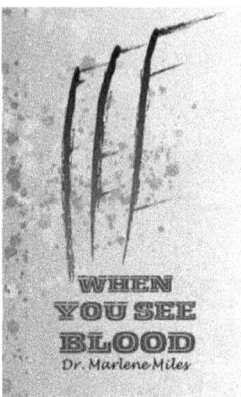

The Wilderness Romance *(series)*

- *The Social Wilderness*
- *The Sexual Wilderness*
- *The Spiritual Wilderness*

Without Form: Finish the Work

https://a.co/d/6WBevhv

Series

The Fold (a series on Godly finances)
https://a.co/d/4hz3unj

Soul Prosperity Series https://a.co/d/bz2M42q

Spirit Spouse books

https://a.co/d/9VehDSo

https://a.co/d/97sKOwm

 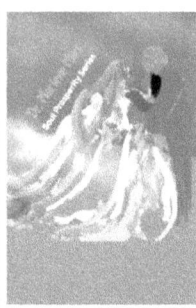

Thieves of Darkness series

Triangular Powers https://a.co/d/aUCjAWC

Upgrade (series) *How to Get Out of Survival Mode*
https://a.co/d/aTERhX0

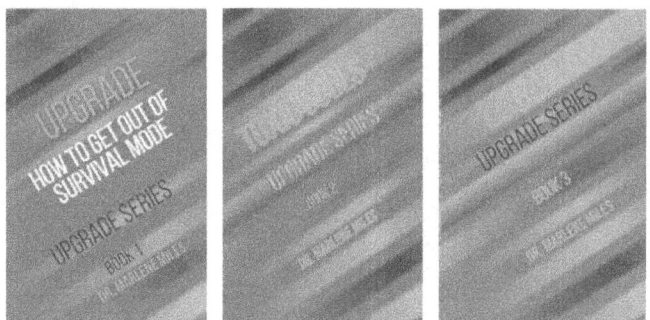

www.ingramcontent.com/pod-product-compliance
Lightning Source LLC
Chambersburg PA
CBHW070540080426
42453CB00030B/2210